THE TEMPEST.

MR. VVILLIAM

SHAKESPEARE'S

THE

TEMPEST.

A

COMEDY,

Published according to the True Originall copy.

LONDON:

Published by PENGUIN BOOKS,

2016.

PENGUIN CLASSICS

UK | USA | Canada | Ireland | Australia
India | New Zealand | South Africa

Penguin Books is part of the Penguin Random House group of companies
whose addresses can be found at global.penguinrandomhouse.com.

Penguin
Random House
UK

This edition first published 2016

I

Text based on the First Folio, typographical arrangement
copyright © Internet Shakespeare Editions 2016

Set in Storm John Baskerville Text
Designed and typeset by David Pearson
Printed in Great Britain by Clays Ltd, St Ives plc

ISBN: 978-0-241-25507-0

www.greenpenguin.co.uk

MIX
Paper from
responsible sources
FSC® C018179

Penguin Random House is committed to a
sustainable future for our business, our readers
and our planet. This book is made from Forest
Stewardship Council® certified paper.

THE

TEMPEST.

A tempestuous noise of Thunder and Lightning heard:
Enter a Ship-master, and a Boteswaine.

Master. Bote-swaine.

Botes. Heere Master: What cheere?

Mast. Good: Speake to th'Mariners: fall too't, yarely, or
we run our selues a ground, bestirre, bestirre.   *Exit.*

Enter Mariners.

Botes. Heigh my hearts, cheerely, cheerely my harts: yare,
yare: Take in the toppe-sale: Tend to th'Masters whistle:
Blow till thou burst thy winde, if roome enough.

Enter Alonso, Sebastian, Anthonio, Ferdinando,
Gonzalo, and others.

Alon. Good Boteswaine haue care: where's the Master?
Play the men.

Botes. I pray now keepe below.

Anth. Where is the Master, Boson?

Botes. Do you not heare him? you marre our labour, Keepe
your Cabines: you do assist the storme.

Gonz. Nay, good be patient.

Botes. When the Sea is: hence, what cares these roarers for
the name of King? to Cabine; silence: trouble vs not.

Gon. Good, yet remember whom thou hast aboord.

Botes. None that I more loue then my selfe. You are a Counsellor, if you can command these Elements to silence, and worke the peace of the present, wee will not hand a rope more, vse your authoritie: If you cannot, giue thankes you haue liu'd so long, and make your selfe readie in your Cabine for the mischance of the houre, if it so hap. Cheerely good hearts: out of our way I say. *Exit.*

Gon. I haue great comfort from this fellow: methinks he hath no drowning marke vpon him, his complexion is perfect Gallowes: stand fast good Fate to his hanging, make the rope of his destiny our cable, for our owne doth little aduantage: If he be not borne to bee hang'd, our case is miserable. *Exit.*

Enter Boteswaine.

Botes. Downe with the top-Mast: yare, lower, lower, bring her to Try with Maine-course. A plague—-

A cry within. Enter Sebastian, Anthonio & Gonzalo.
vpon this howling: they are lowder then the weather, or our office: yet againe? What do you heere? Shal we giue ore and drowne, haue you a minde to sinke?

Sebas. A poxe o'your throat, you bawling, blasphemous incharitable Dog.

Botes. Worke you then.

Anth. Hang cur, hang, you whoreson insolent Noyse-maker, we are lesse afraid to be drownde, then thou art.

Gonz. I'le warrant him for drowning, though the Ship were no stronger then a Nutt-shell, and as leaky as an vn-stanched wench.

Botes. Lay her a hold, a hold, set her two courses off to Sea againe, lay her off.

Enter Mariners wet.

Mari. All lost, to prayers, to prayers, all lost.

Botes. What must our mouths be cold?

Gonz. The King, and Prince, at prayers, let's assist them, for our case is as theirs.

Sebas. I'am out of patience.

An. We are meerly cheated of our liues by drunkards, This wide-chopt-rascall, would thou mightst lye drowning the washing of ten Tides.

Gonz. Hee'l be hang'd yet,
Though euery drop of water sweare against it,
And gape at widst to glut him.

A confused noyse within.

Mercy on vs.
We split, we split, Farewell my wife, and children,
Farewell brother: we split, we split, we split.

Anth. Let's all sinke with' King

Seb. Let's take leaue of him.   *Exit.*

Gonz. Now would I giue a thousand furlongs of Sea, for an Acre of barren ground: Long heath, Browne firrs, any thing; the wills aboue be done, but I would faine dye a dry death.   *Exit.*

Scena Secunda.

Enter Prospero and Miranda.

Mira. If by your Art (my deerest father) you haue
Put the wild waters in this Rore; alay them:
The skye it seemes would powre down stinking pitch,
But that the Sea, mounting to th' welkins cheeke,
Dashes the fire out. Oh! I haue suffered
With those that I saw suffer: A braue vessell
(Who had no doubt some noble creature in her)
Dash'd all to peeces: O the cry did knocke
Against my very heart: poore soules, they perish'd.
Had I byn any God of power, I would
Haue suncke the Sea within the Earth, or ere
It should the good Ship so haue swallow'd, and
The fraughting Soules within her.

Pros. Be collected,
No more amazement: Tell your pitteous heart
there's no harme done.

Mira. O woe, the day.

Pros. No harme:
I haue done nothing, but in care of thee
(Of thee my deere one; thee my daughter) who
Art ignorant of what thou art. naught knowing
Of whence I am: nor that I am more better
Then *Prospero*, Master of a full poore cell,
And thy no greater Father.

Mira. More to know
Did neuer medle with my thoughts.

Pros. 'Tis time

4

I should informe thee farther: Lend thy hand
And plucke my Magick garment from me: So,
Lye there my Art: wipe thou thine eyes, haue comfort,
The direfull spectacle of the wracke which touch'd
The very vertue of compassion in thee:
I haue with such prouision in mine Art
So safely ordered, that there is no soule
No not so much perdition as an hayre
Betid to any creature in the vessell
Which thou heardst cry, which thou saw'st sinke: Sit downe,
For thou must now know farther.

   Mira. You haue often
Begun to tell me what I am, but stopt
And left me to a bootelesse Inquisition,
Concluding, stay: not yet.

   Pros. The howr's now come
The very minute byds thee ope thine eare,
Obey, and be attentiue. Canst thou remember
A time before we came vnto this Cell?
I doe not thinke thou canst, for then thou was't not
Out three yeeres old.

   Mira. Certainely Sir, I can.

   Pros. By what? by any other house, or person?
Of any thing the Image, tell me, that
Hath kept with thy remembrance.

   Mira. 'Tis farre off:
And rather like a dreame, then an assurance
That my remembrance warrants: Had I not
Fowre, or fiue women once, that tended me?

   Pros. Thou hadst; and more *Miranda:* But how is it
That this liues in thy minde? What seest thou els
In the dark-backward and Abisme of Time?

Yf thou remembrest ought ere thou cam'st here,
How thou cam'st here thou maist.

Mira. But that I doe not.

Pros. Twelue yere since (*Miranda*) twelue yere since,
Thy father was the Duke of *Millaine* and
A Prince of power:

Mira. Sir, are not you my Father?

Pros. Thy Mother was a peece of vertue, and
She said thou wast my daughter; and thy father
Was Duke of *Millaine*, and his onely heire,
And Princesse; no worse Issued.

Mira. O the heauens,
What fowle play had we, that we came from thence?
Or blessed was't we did?

Pros. Both, both my Girle.
By fowle-play (as thou saist) were we heau'd thence,
But blessedly holpe hither.

Mira. O my heart bleedes
To thinke oth' teene that I haue turn'd you to,
Which is from my remembrance, please you, farther;

Pros. My brother and thy vncle, call'd *Anthonio*:
I pray thee marke me, that a brother should
Be so perfidious: he, whom next thy selfe
Of all the world I lou'd, and to him put
The mannage of my state, as at that time
Through all the signories it was the first,
And *Prospero*, the prime Duke, being so reputed
In dignity; and for the liberall Artes,
Without a paralell; those being all my studie,
The Gouernment I cast vpon my brother,
And to my State grew stranger, being transported
And rapt in secret studies, thy false vncle

(Do'st thou attend me?)

Mira. Sir, most heedefully.

Pros. Being once perfected how to graunt suites,
how to deny them: who t'aduance, and who
To trash for ouer-topping; new created
The creatures that were mine, I say, or chang'd 'em,
Or els new form'd 'em; hauing both the key,
Of Officer, and office, set all hearts i'th state
To what tune pleas'd his eare, that now he was
The Iuy which had hid my princely Trunck,
And suckt my verdure out on't: Thou attend'st not?

Mira. O good Sir, I doe.

Pros. I pray thee marke me:
I thus neglecting worldly ends, all dedicated
To closenes, and the bettering of my mind
with that, which but by being so retir'd
Ore-priz'd all popular rate: in my false brother
Awak'd an euill nature, and my trust
Like a good parent, did beget of him
A falsehood in it's contrarie, as great
As my trust was, which had indeede no limit,
A confidence sans bound. He being thus Lorded,
Not onely with what my reuenew yeelded,
But what my power might els exact. Like one
Who hauing into truth, by telling of it,
Made such a synner of his memorie
To credite his owne lie, he did beleeue
He was indeed the Duke, out o'th' Substitution
And executing th'outward face of Roialtie
With all prerogatiue: hence his Ambition growing:
Do'st thou heare?

Mira. Your tale, Sir, would cure deafenesse.

Pros. To haue no Schreene between this part he plaid,
And him he plaid it for, he needes will be
Absolute *Millaine*, Me (poore man) my Librarie
Was Dukedome large enough: of temporall roalties
He thinks me now incapable. Confederates
(so drie he was for Sway) with King of *Naples*
To giue him Annuall tribute, doe him homage
Subiect his Coronet, to his Crowne and bend
The Dukedom yet vnbow'd (alas poore *Millaine*)
To most ignoble stooping.
   Mira. Oh the heauens:
   Pros. Marke his condition, and th'euent, then tell me
If this might be a brother.
   Mira. I should sinne
To thinke but Noblie of my Grand-mother,
Good wombes haue borne bad sonnes.
   Pro. Now the Condition.
This King of *Naples* being an Enemy
To me inueterate, hearkens my Brothers suit,
Which was, That he in lieu o'th' premises,
Of homage, and I know not how much Tribute,
Should presently extirpate me and mine
Out of the Dukedome, and confer faire *Millaine*
With all the Honors, on my brother: Whereon
A treacherous Armie leuied, one mid-night
Fated to th' purpose, did *Anthonio* open
The gates of *Millaine*, and ith' dead of darkenesse
The ministers for th' purpose hurried thence
Me, and thy crying selfe.
   Mir. Alack, for pitty:
I not remembring how I cride out then
Will cry it ore againe: it is a hint

That wrings mine eyes too't.

   Pro. Heare a little further,
And then I'le bring thee to the present businesse
Which now's vpon's: without the which, this Story
Were most impertinent.

   Mir. Wherefore did they not
That howre destroy vs?

   Pro. Well demanded, wench:
My Tale prouokes that question: Deare, they durst not,
So deare the loue my people bore me: nor set
A marke so bloudy on the businesse; but
With colours fairer, painted their foule ends.
In few, they hurried vs a-boord a Barke,
Bore vs some Leagues to Sea, where they prepared
A rotten carkasse of a Butt, not rigg'd,
Nor tackle, sayle, nor mast, the very rats
Instinctiuely haue quit it: There they hoyst vs
To cry to th' Sea, that roard to vs; to sigh
To th' windes, whose pitty sighing backe againe
Did vs but louing wrong.

   Mir. Alack, what trouble
Was I then to you?

   Pro. O, a Cherubin
Thou was't that did preserue me; Thou didst smile,
Infused with a fortitude from heauen,
When I haue deck'd the sea with drops full salt,
Vnder my burthen groan'd, which rais'd in me
An vndergoing stomacke, to beare vp
Against what should ensue.

   Mir. How came we a shore?

   Pro. By prouidence diuine,
Some food, we had, and some fresh water, that

A noble *Neopolitan Gonzalo*
Out of his Charity, (who being then appointed
Master of this designe) did giue vs, with
Rich garments, linnens, stuffs, and necessaries
Which since haue steeded much, so of his gentlenesse
Knowing I lou'd my bookes, he furnishd me
From mine owne Library, with volumes, that
I prize aboue my Dukedome.

   Mir. Would I might
But euer see that man.

   Pro. Now I arise,
Sit still, and heare the last of our sea-sorrow:
Heere in this Iland we arriu'd, and heere
Haue I, thy Schoolemaster, made thee more profit
Then other Princesse can, that haue more time
For vainer howres; and Tutors, not so carefull.

   Mir. Heuens thank you for't. And now I pray you Sir,
For still 'tis beating in my minde; your reason
For raysing this Sea-storme?

   Pro. Know thus far forth,
By accident most strange, bountifull *Fortune*
(Now my deere Lady) hath mine enemies
Brought to this shore: And by my prescience
I finde my *Zenith* doth depend vpon
A most auspitious starre, whose influence
If now I court not, but omit; my fortunes
Will euer after droope: Heare cease more questions,
Thou art inclinde to sleepe: 'tis a good dulnesse,
And giue it way: I know thou canst not chuse:
Come away, Seruant, come; I am ready now,
Approach my *Ariel*. Come.

              Enter Ariel.

Ari. All haile, great Master, graue Sir, haile: I come
To answer thy best pleasure; be't to fly,
To swim, to diue into the fire: to ride
On the curld clowds: to thy strong bidding, taske
Ariel, and all his Qualitie.

Pro. Hast thou, Spirit,
Performd to point, the Tempest that I bad thee.

Ar. To euery Article.
I boorded the Kings ship: now on the Beake,
Now in the Waste, the Decke, in euery Cabyn,
I flam'd amazement, sometime I'ld diuide
And burne in many places; on the Top-mast,
The Yards and Bore-spritt, would I flame distinctly,
Then meete, and ioyne. *Ioues* Lightning, the precursers
O'th dreadfull Thunder-claps more momentarie
And sight out-running were not; the fire, and cracks
Of sulphurous roaring, the most mighty *Neptune*
Seeme to besiege, and make his bold waues tremble,
Yea, his dread Trident shake.

Pro. My braue Spirit,
Who was so firme, so constant, that this coyle
Would not infect his reason?

Ar. Not a soule
But felt a Feauer of the madde, and plaid
Some tricks of desperation; all but Mariners
Plung'd in the foaming bryne, and quit the vessell;
Then all a fire with me the Kings sonne *Ferdinand*
With haire vp-staring (then like reeds, not haire)
Was the first man that leapt; cride hell is empty,
And all the Diuels are heere.

Pro. Why that's my spirit:
But was not this nye shore?

Ar. Close by, my Master.

Pro. But are they (*Ariell*) safe?

Ar. Not a haire perishd:
On their sustaining garments not a blemish,
But fresher then before: and as thou badst me,
In troops I haue dispersd them 'bout the Isle:
The Kings sonne haue I landed by himselfe,
Whom I left cooling of the Ayre with sighes,
In an odde Angle of the Isle, and sitting
His armes in this sad knot.

Pro. Of the Kings ship,
The Marriners, say how thou hast disposd,
And all the rest o'th' Fleete?

Ar. Safely in harbour
Is the Kings shippe, in the deepe Nooke, where once
Thou calldst me vp at midnight to fetch dewe
From the still-vext *Bermoothes*, there she's hid;
The Marriners all vnder hatches stowed,
Who, with a Charme ioynd to their suffred labour
I haue left asleep: and for the rest o'th' Fleet
(Which I dispers'd) they all haue met againe,
And are vpon the *Mediterranian* Flote
Bound sadly home for *Naples*,
Supposing that they saw the Kings ship wrackt,
And his great person perish.

Pro. Ariel, thy charge
Exactly is perform'd; but there's more worke:
What is the time o'th'day?

Ar. Past the mid season.

Pro. At least two Glasses: the time 'twixt six & now
Must by vs both be spent most preciously.

Ar. Is there more toyle? Since y^u dost giue me pains,

Let me remember thee what thou hast promis'd,
Which is not yet perform'd me.

Pro. How now? moodie?
What is't thou canst demand?

Ar. My Libertie.

Pro. Before the time be out? no more:

Ar. I prethee,
Remember I haue done thee worthy seruice,
Told thee no lyes, made thee no mistakings, serv'd
Without or grudge, or grumblings; thou did promise
To bate me a full yeere.

Pro. Do'st thou forget
From what a torment I did free thee?

Ar. No.

Pro. Thou do'st: & thinkst it much to tread yᵉ Ooze
Of the salt deepe;
To run vpon the sharpe winde of the North,
To doe me businesse in the veines o'th' earth
When it is bak'd with frost.

Ar. I doe not Sir.

Pro. Thou liest, malignant Thing: hast thou forgot
The fowle Witch *Sycorax*, who with Age and Enuy
Was growne into a hoope? hast thou forgot her?

Ar. No Sir.

Pro. Thou hast: where was she born? speak: tell me:

Ar. Sir, in *Argier*.

Pro. Oh, was she so: I must
Once in a moneth recount what thou hast bin,
Which thou forgetst. This damn'd Witch *Sycorax*
For mischiefes manifold, and sorceries terrible
To enter humane hearing, from *Argier*
Thou know'st was banish'd: for one thing she did

They wold not take her life: Is not this true?

Ar. I, Sir.

Pro. This blew ey'd hag, was hither brought with child,
And here was left by th' Saylors; thou my slaue,
As thou reportst thy selfe, was then her seruant,
And for thou wast a Spirit too delicate
To act her earthy, and abhord commands,
Refusing her grand hests, she did confine thee
By helpe of her more potent Ministers,
And in her most vnmittigable rage,
Into a clouen Pyne, within which rift
Imprison'd, thou didst painefully remaine
A dozen yeeres: within which space she di'd,
And left thee there: where thou didst vent thy groanes
As fast as Mill-wheeles strike: Then was this Island
(Saue for the Son, that he did littour heere,
A frekelld whelpe, hag-borne) not honour'd with
A humane shape.

Ar. Yes: *Caliban* her sonne.

Pro. Dull thing, I say so: he, that *Caliban*
Whom now I keepe in seruice, thou best know'st
What torment I did finde thee in; thy grones
Did make wolues howle, and penetrate the breasts
Of euer-angry Beares; it was a torment
To lay vpon the damn'd, which *Sycorax*
Could not againe vndoe: it was mine Art,
When I arriu'd, and heard thee, that made gape
The Pyne, and let thee out.

Ar. I thanke thee Master.

Pro. If thou more murmur'st, I will rend an Oake
And peg-thee in his knotty entrailes, till
Thou hast howl'd away twelue winters.

Ar. Pardon, Master,
I will be correspondent to command
And doe my spryting, gently.

Pro. Doe so: and after two daies
I will discharge thee.

Ar. That's my noble Master:
What shall I doe? say what? what shall I doe?

Pro. Goe make thy selfe like a Nymph o'th' Sea,
Be subiect to no sight but thine, and mine: inuisible
To euery eye-ball else: goe take this shape
And hither come in't: goe: hence
With diligence.   *Exit.*

Pro. Awake, deere hart awake, thou hast slept well,
Awake.

Mir. The strangenes of your story, put
Heauinesse in me.

Pro. Shake it off: Come on,
Wee'll visit *Caliban*, my slaue, who neuer
Yeelds vs kinde answere.

Mir. 'Tis a villaine Sir, I doe not loue to looke on.

Pro. But as 'tis
We cannot misse him: he do's make our fire,
Fetch in our wood, and serues in Offices
That profit vs: What hoa: slaue: *Caliban*:
Thou Earth, thou: speake.

Cal. within. There's wood enough within.

Pro. Come forth I say, there's other busines for thee:
Come thou Tortoys, when?

> *Enter Ariel like a water-Nymph.*

Fine apparision: my queint *Ariel*,
Hearke in thine eare.

Ar. My Lord, it shall be done.   *Exit.*

Pro. Thou poysonous slaue, got by yᵉ diuell himselfe
Vpon thy wicked Dam; come forth.

Enter Caliban.

Cal. As wicked dewe, as ere my mother brush'd
With Rauens feather from vnwholesome Fen
Drop on you both: A Southwest blow on yee,
And blister you all ore.

Pro. For this be sure, to night thou shalt haue cramps,
Side-stitches, that shall pen thy breath vp, Vrchins
Shall for that vast of night, that they may worke
All exercise on thee: thou shalt be pinch'd
As thicke as hony-combe, each pinch more stinging
Then Bees that made 'em.

Cal. I must eat my dinner:
This Island's mine by *Sycorax* my mother,
Which thou tak'st from me: when thou cam'st first
Thou stroakst me, & made much of me: wouldst giue me
Water with berries in't: and teach me how
To name the bigger Light, and how the lesse
That burne by day, and night: and then I lou'd thee
And shew'd thee all the qualities o'th' Isle,
The fresh Springs, Brine-pits; barren place and fertill,
Curs'd be I that did so: All the Charmes
Of *Sycorax*: Toades, Beetles, Batts light on you:
For I am all the Subiects that you haue,
Which first was min owne King: and here you sty-me
In this hard Rocke, whiles you doe keepe from me
The rest o'th' Island.

Pro. Thou most lying slaue,
Whom stripes may moue, not kindnes: I haue vs'd thee
(Filth as thou art) with humane care, and lodg'd thee
In mine owne Cell, till thou didst seeke to violate

The honor of my childe.

   Cal. Oh ho, oh ho, would't had bene done:
Thou didst preuent me, I had peopel'd else
This Isle with *Calibans*.

   Mira. Abhorred Slaue,
Which any print of goodnesse wilt not take,
Being capable of all ill: I pittied thee,
Took pains to make thee speak, taught thee each houre
One thing or other: when thou didst not (Sauage)
Know thine owne meaning; but wouldst gabble, like
A thing most brutish, I endow'd thy purposes
With words that made them knowne: But thy vild race
(Tho thou didst learn) had that in't, which good natures
Could not abide to be with; therefore wast thou
Deseruedly confin'd into this Rocke, who hadst
Deseru'd more then a prison.

   Cal. You taught me Language, and my profit on't
Is, I know how to curse: the red-plague rid you
For learning me your language.

   Pros. Hag-seed, hence:
Fetch vs in Fewell, and be quicke thou'rt best
To answer other businesse: shrug'st thou (Malice)
If thou neglectst, or dost vnwillingly
What I command, Ile racke thee with old Crampes,
Fill all thy bones with Aches, make thee rore,
That beasts shall tremble at thy dyn.

   Cal. No, 'pray thee.
I must obey, his Art is of such pow'r,
It would controll my Dams god *Setebos*,
And make a vassaile of him.

   Pro. So slaue, hence.   *Exit Cal.*
     Enter Ferdinand & Ariel, inuisible playing & singing.

Ariel Song. *Come vnto these yellow sands,*
   and then take hands:
  Curtsied when you haue, and kist
   the wilde waues whist: Foote it featly heere, and
  there, and sweete Sprights beare
   the burthen.   Burthen dispersedly.
  Harke, harke, bowgh wawgh: the watch-Dogges barke,
   bowgh-wawgh.
   Ar. Hark, hark, I heare, the straine of strutting
  Chanticlere
   cry cockadidle-dowe.

 Fer. Where shold this Musick be? I'th aire, or th'earth?
It sounds no more: and sure it waytes vpon
Some God 'oth' Iland, sitting on a banke,
Weeping againe the King my Fathers wracke.
This Musicke crept by me vpon the waters,
Allaying both their fury, and my passion
With it's sweet ayre: thence I haue follow'd it
(Or it hath drawne me rather) but 'tis gone.
No, it begins againe.

 Ariell Song. *Full fadom fiue thy Father lies,*
   Of his bones are Corrall made:
   Those are pearles that were his eies,
   Nothing of him that doth fade,
   But doth suffer a Sea-change
   Into something rich, & strange:
   Sea-Nimphs hourly ring his knell.
         Burthen: ding dong.
  Harke now I heare them, ding-dong bell.

 Fer. The Ditty do's remember my drown'd father,
This is no mortall busines, nor no sound
That the earth owes: I heare it now aboue me.

Pro. The fringed Curtaines of thine eye aduance,
And say what thou see'st yond.

Mira. What is't a Spirit?
Lord, how it lookes about: Beleeue me sir,
It carries a braue forme. But 'tis a spirit.

Pro. No wench, it eats, and sleeps, & hath such senses
As we haue: such. This Gallant which thou seest
Was in the wracke: and but hee's something stain'd
With greefe (that's beauties canker) y^u might'st call him
A goodly person: he hath lost his fellowes,
And strayes about to finde 'em.

Mir. I might call him
A thing diuine, for nothing naturall
I euer saw so Noble.

Pro. It goes on I see
As my soule prompts it: Spirit, fine spirit, Ile free thee
Within two dayes for this.

Fer. Most sure the Goddesse
On whom these ayres attend: Vouchsafe my pray'r
May know if you remaine vpon this Island,
And that you will some good instruction giue
How I may beare me heere: my prime request
(Which I do last pronounce) is (O you wonder)
If you be Mayd, or no?

Mir. No wonder Sir,
But certainly a Mayd.

Fer. My Language? Heauens:
I am the best of them that speake this speech,
Were I but where 'tis spoken.

Pro. How? the best?
What wer't thou if the King of *Naples* heard thee?

Fer. A single thing, as I am now, that wonders

To heare thee speake of *Naples:* he do's heare me,
And that he do's, I weepe: my selfe am *Naples,*
Who, with mine eyes (neuer since at ebbe) beheld
The King my Father wrack't.

   Mir. Alacke, for mercy.

   Fer. Yes faith, & all his Lords, the Duke of *Millaine*
And his braue sonne, being twaine.

   Pro. The Duke of *Millaine*
And his more brauer daughter, could controll thee
If now 'twere fit to do't: At the first sight
They haue chang'd eyes: Delicate *Ariel,*
Ile set thee free for this. A word good Sir,
I feare you haue done your selfe some wrong: A word.

   Mir. Why speakes my father so vngently? This
Is the third man that ere I saw: the first
That ere I sigh'd for: pitty moue my father
To be enclin'd my way.

   Fer. O, if a Virgin,
And your affection not gone forth, Ile make you
The Queene of *Naples.*

   Pro. Soft sir, one word more.
They are both in eythers pow'rs: But this swift busines
I must vneasie make, least too light winning
Make the prize light. One word more: I charge thee
That thou attend me: Thou do'st heere vsurpe
The name thou ow'st not, and hast put thy selfe
Vpon this Island, as a spy, to win it
From me, the Lord on't.

   Fer. No, as I am a man.

   Mir. Ther's nothing ill, can dwell in such a Temple,
If the ill-spirit haue so fayre a house,
Good things will striue to dwell with't.

Pro. Follow me.

Speake not you for him: hee's a Traitor: come,
Ile manacle thy necke and feete together:
Sea water shalt thou drinke: thy food shall be
The fresh-brooke Mussels, wither'd roots, and huskes
Wherein the Acorne cradled. Follow.

Fer. No,
I will resist such entertainment, till
Mine enemy ha's more pow'r.

               He drawes, and is charmed from mouing.

Mira. O deere Father,
Make not too rash a triall of him, for
Hee's gentle, and not fearfull.

Pros. What I say,
My foote my Tutor? Put thy sword vp Traitor,
Who mak'st a shew, but dar'st not strike: thy conscience
Is so possest with guilt: Come, from thy ward,
For I can heere disarme thee with this sticke,
And make thy weapon drop.

Mira. Beseech you Father.

Pros. Hence: hang not on my garments.

Mira. Sir haue pity,
Ile be his surety.

Pros. Silence: One word more
Shall make me chide thee, if not hate thee: What,
An aduocate for an Impostor? Hush:
Thou think'st there is no more such shapes as he,
(Hauing seene but him and *Caliban:*) Foolish wench,
To th'most of men, this is a *Caliban*,
And they to him are Angels.

Mira. My affections
Are then most humble: I haue no ambition

To see a goodlier man.

 Pros. Come on, obey:
Thy Nerues are in their infancy againe.
And haue no vigour in them.

 Fer. So they are:
My spirits, as in a dreame, are all bound vp:
My Fathers losse, the weakenesse which I feele,
The wracke of all my friends, nor this mans threats,
To whom I am subdude, are but light to me,
Might I but through my prison once a day
Behold this Mayd: all corners else o'th' Earth
Let liberty make vse of: space enough
Haue I in such a prison.

 Pros. It workes: Come on.
Thou hast done well, fine *Ariell:* follow me,
Harke what thou else shalt do mee.

 Mira. Be of comfort,
My Fathers of a better nature (Sir)
Then he appeares by speech: this is vnwonted
Which now came from him.

 Pros. Thou shalt be as free
As mountaine windes; but then exactly do
All points of my command.

 Ariell. To th'syllable.

 Pros. Come follow: speake not for him.   *Exeunt.*

Actus Secundus. Scœna Prima.

Enter Alonso, Sebastian, Anthonio, Gonzalo,
Adrian, Francisco, and others.

Gonz. Beseech you Sir, be merry; you haue cause,
(So haue we all) of ioy; for our escape
Is much beyond our losse; our hint of woe
Is common, euery day, some Saylors wife,
The Masters of some Merchant, and the Merchant
Haue iust our Theame of woe: But for the miracle,
(I meane our preseruation) few in millions
Can speake like vs: then wisely (good Sir) weigh
Our sorrow, with our comfort.

Alons. Prethee peace.

Seb. He receiues comfort like cold porredge.

Ant. The Visitor will not giue him ore so.

Seb. Looke, hee's winding vp the watch of his wit, By and
by it will strike.

Gon. Sir.

Seb. One: Tell.

Gon. When euery greefe is entertaind,
That's offer'd comes to th'entertainer.

Seb. A dollor.

Gon. Dolour comes to him indeed, you haue spoken truer
then you purpos'd.

Seb. You haue taken it wiselier then I meant you should.

Gon. Therefore my Lord.

Ant. Fie, what a spend-thrift is he of his tongue.

Alon. I pre-thee spare.

23

Gon. Well, I haue done: But yet

Seb. He will be talking.

Ant. Which, of he, or Adrian, for a good wager,
First begins to crow?

Seb. The old Cocke.

Ant. The Cockrell.

Seb. Done: The wager?

Ant. A Laughter.

Seb. A match.

Adr. Though this Island seeme to be desert.

Seb. Ha, ha, ha.

Ant. So: you'r paid.

Adr. Vninhabitable, and almost inaccessible.

Seb. Yet

Adr. Yet

Ant. He could not misse't.

Adr. It must needs be of subtle, tender, and delicate temperance.

Ant. *Temperance* was a delicate wench.

Seb. I, and a subtle, as he most learnedly deliuer'd.

Adr. The ayre breathes vpon vs here most sweetly.

Seb. As if it had Lungs, and rotten ones.

Ant. Or, as 'twere perfum'd by a Fen.

Gon. Heere is euery thing aduantageous to life.

Ant. True, saue meanes to liue.

Seb. Of that there's none, or little.

Gon. How lush and lusty the grasse lookes?
How greene?

Ant. The ground indeed is tawny.

Seb. With an eye of greene in't.

Ant. He misses not much.

Seb. No: he doth but mistake the truth totally.

Gon. But the rariety of it is, which is indeed almost beyond credit.

Seb. As many voucht rarieties are.

Gon. That our Garments being (as they were) drencht in the Sea, hold notwithstanding their freshnesse and glosses, being rather new dy'de then stain'd with salte water.

Ant. If but one of his pockets could speake, would it not say he lyes?

Seb. I, or very falsely pocket vp his report.

Gon. Me thinkes our garments are now as fresh as when we put them on first in Affricke, at the marriage of the kings faire daughter *Claribel* to the king of *Tunis*.

Seb. 'Twas a sweet marriage, and we prosper well in our returne.

Adri. *Tunis* was neuer grac'd before with such a Paragon to their Queene.

Gon. Not since widdow *Dido's* time.

Ant. Widow? A pox o'that: how came that Widdow in? Widdow *Dido!*

Seb. What if he had said Widdower *Æneas* too? Good Lord, how you take it?

Adri. Widdow *Dido* said you? You make me study of that: She was of *Carthage*, not of *Tunis*.

Gon. This *Tunis* Sir was *Carthage*.

Adri. *Carthage?*

Gon. I assure you *Carthage*.

Ant. His word is more then the miraculous Harpe.

Seb. He hath rais'd the wall, and houses too.

Ant. What impossible matter wil he make easy next?

Seb. I thinke hee will carry this Island home in his pocket, and giue it his sonne for an Apple.

Ant. And sowing the kernels of it in the Sea, bring forth

more Islands.

Gon. I.

Ant. Why in good time.

Gon. Sir, we were talking, that our garments seeme now as fresh as when we were at *Tunis* at the marriage of your daughter, who is now Queene.

Ant. And the rarest that ere came there.

Seb. Bate (I beseech you) widdow *Dido*.

Ant. O Widdow *Dido*? I, Widdow *Dido*.

Gon. Is not Sir my doublet as fresh as the first day I wore it? I meane in a sort.

Ant. That sort was well fish'd for.

Gon. When I wore it at your daughters marriage.

Alon. You cram these words into mine eares, against
the stomacke of my sense: would I had neuer
Married my daughter there: For comming thence
My sonne is lost, and (in my rate) she too,
Who is so farre from *Italy* remoued,
I ne're againe shall see her: O thou mine heire
Of *Naples* and of *Millaine*, what strange fish
Hath made his meale on thee?

Fran. Sir he may liue,
I saw him beate the surges vnder him,
And ride vpon their backes; he trod the water
Whose enmity he flung aside: and brested
The surge most swolne that met him: his bold head
'Boue the contentious waues he kept. and oared
Himselfe with his good armes in lusty stroke
To th'shore; that ore his waue-worne basis bowed
As stooping to releeue him: I not doubt
He came aliue to Land.

Alon. No, no, hee's gone.

Seb. Sir you may thank your selfe for this great losse,
That would not blesse our Europe with your daughter,
But rather loose her to an Affrican,
Where she at least, is banish'd from your eye,
Who hath cause to wet the greefe on't.

Alon. Pre-thee peace.

Seb. You were kneel'd too, & importun'd otherwise
By all of vs: and the faire soule her selfe
Waigh'd betweene loathnesse, and obedience, at
Which end o'th'beame should bow: we haue lost your son,
I feare for euer: *Millaine* and *Naples* haue
Mo widdowes in them of this businesse making,
Then we bring men to comfort them:
The faults your owne.

Alon. So is the deer'st oth' losse.

Gon. My Lord *Sebastian*,
The truth you speake doth lacke some gentlenesse,
And time to speake it in: you rub the sore,
When you should bring the plaister.

Seb. Very well.

Ant. And most Chirurgeonly.

Gon. It is foule weather in vs all, good Sir,
When you are cloudy.

Seb. Fowle weather?

Ant. Very foule.

Gon. Had I plantation of this Isle my Lord.

Ant. Hee'd sow't vvith Nettle-seed.

Seb. Or dockes, or Mallowes.

Gon. And were the King on't, what vvould I do?

Seb. Scape being drunke, for want of Wine.

Gon. I'th'Commonwealth I vvould (by contraries)
Execute all things: For no kinde of Trafficke

Would I admit: No name of Magistrate:
Letters should not be knowne: Riches, pouerty,
And vse of seruice, none: Contract, Succession,
Borne, bound of Land, Tilth, Vineyard none:
No vse of Mettall, Corne, or Wine, or Oyle:
No occupation, all men idle, all:
And Women too, but innocent and pure:
No Soueraignty.

 Seb. Yet he vvould be King on't.

 Ant. The latter end of his Common-wealth forgets the be-
ginning.

 Gon. All things in common Nature should produce
Without sweat or endeuour: Treason, fellony,
Sword, Pike, Knife, Gun, or neede of any Engine
Would I not haue: but Nature should bring forth
Of it owne kinde, all foyzon, all abundance
To feed my innocent people.

 Seb. No marrying 'mong his subiects?

 Ant. None (man) all idle; Whores and knaues,

 Gon. I vvould vvith such perfection gouerne Sir:
T'Excell the Golden Age.

 Seb. 'Saue his Maiesty.

 Ant. Long liue *Gonzalo*.

 Gon. And do you marke me, Sir?

 Alon. Pre-thee no more: thou dost talke nothing to me.

 Gon. I do vvell beleeue your Highnesse, and did it to
minister occasion to these Gentlemen, who are of such sen-
sible and nimble Lungs, that they alwayes vse to laugh at
nothing.

 Ant. 'Twas you vve laugh'd at.

 Gon. Who, in this kind of merry fooling am nothing to
you: so you may continue, and laugh at nothing still.

Ant. What a blow vvas there giuen?

Seb. And it had not falne flat-long.

Gon. You are Gentlemen of braue mettal: you would lift the Moone out of her spheare, if she would continue in it fiue weekes vvithout changing.

Enter Ariell playing solemne Musicke.

Seb. We vvould so, and then go a Bat-fowling.

Ant. Nay good my Lord, be not angry.

Gon. No I warrant you, I vvill not aduenture my discretion so weakly: Will you laugh me asleepe, for I am very heauy.

Ant. Go sleepe, and heare vs.

Alon. What, all so soone asleepe? I wish mine eyes
Would (with themselues) shut vp my thoughts,
I finde they are inclin'd to do so.

Seb. Please you Sir,
Do not omit the heauy offer of it:
It sildome visits sorrow, when it doth, it is a Comforter.

Ant. We two my Lord, will guard your person,
While you take your rest, and watch your safety.

Alon. Thanke you: Wondrous heauy.

Seb. What a strange drowsines possesses them?

Ant. It is the quality o'th'Clymate.

Seb. Why
Doth it not then our eye-lids sinke? I finde
Not my selfe dispos'd to sleep.

Ant. Nor I, my spirits are nimble:
They fell together all, as by consent
They dropt, as by a Thunder-stroke: what might
Worthy *Sebastian?* O, what might? no more:
And yet, me thinkes I see it in thy face,
What thou should'st be: th'occasion speakes thee, and

My strong imagination see's a Crowne
Dropping vpon thy head.

    Seb. What? art thou waking?

    Ant. Do you not heare me speake?

    Seb. I do, and surely
It is a sleepy Language; and thou speak'st
Out of thy sleepe: What is it thou didst say?
This is a strange repose, to be asleepe
With eyes wide open: standing, speaking, mouing:
And yet so fast asleepe.

    Ant. Noble *Sebastian*,
Thou let'st thy fortune sleepe: die rather: wink'st
Whiles thou art waking.

    Seb. Thou do'st snore distinctly,
There's meaning in thy snores.

    Ant. I am more serious then my custome: you
Must be so too, if heed me: which to do,
Trebbles thee o're.

    Seb. Well: I am standing water.

    Ant. Ile teach you how to flow.

    Seb. Do so: to ebbe
Hereditary Sloth instructs me.

    Ant. O!
If you but knew how you the purpose cherish
Whiles thus you mocke it: how in stripping it
You more inuest it: ebbing men, indeed
(Most often) do so neere the bottome run
By their owne feare, or sloth.

    Seb. 'Pre-thee say on,
The setting of thine eye, and cheeke proclaime
A matter from thee; and a birth, indeed,
Which throwes thee much to yeeld.

Ant. Thus Sir:
Although this Lord of weake remembrance; this
Who shall be of as little memory
When he is earth'd, hath here almost perswaded
(For hee's a Spirit of perswasion, onely
Professes to perswade) the King his sonne's aliue,
'Tis as impossible that hee's vndrown'd,
As he that sleepes heere, swims.

   Seb. I haue no hope
That hee's vndrown'd.

   Ant. O, out of that no hope,
What great hope haue you? No hope that way, Is
Another way so high a hope, that euen
Ambition cannot pierce a winke beyond
But doubt discouery there. Will you grant with me
That *Ferdinand* is drown'd.

   Seb. He's gone.

   Ant. Then tell me, who's the next heire of *Naples?*

   Seb. Claribell.

   Ant. She that is Queene of *Tunis:* she that dwels
Ten leagues beyond mans life: she that from *Naples*
Can haue no note, vnlesse the Sun were post:
The Man i'th Moone's too slow, till new-borne chinnes
Be rough, and Razor-able: She that from whom
We all were sea-swallow'd, though some cast againe,
(And by that destiny) to performe an act
Whereof, what's past is Prologue; what to come
In yours, and my discharge.

   Seb. What stuffe is this? How say you?
'Tis true my brothers daughter's Queene of *Tunis*,
So is she heyre of *Naples*, 'twixt which Regions
There is some space.

Ant. A space, whose eu'ry cubit
Seemes to cry out, how shall that *Claribell*
Measure vs backe to *Naples*? keepe in *Tunis*,
And let *Sebastian* wake. Say, this were death
That now hath seiz'd them, why they were no worse
Then now they are: There be that can rule *Naples*
As well as he that sleepes: Lords, that can prate
As amply, and vnnecessarily
As this *Gonzallo*: I my selfe could make
A Chough of as deepe chat: O, that you bore
The minde that I do; what a sleepe were this
For your aduancement? Do you vnderstand me?

Seb. Me thinkes I do.

Ant. And how do's your content
Tender your owne good fortune?

Seb. I remember
You did supplant your Brothet *Prospero*.

Ant. True:
And looke how well my Garments sit vpon me,
Much feater then before: My Brothers seruants
Were then my fellowes, now they are my men.

Seb. But for your conscience.

Ant. I Sir: where lies that? If 'twere a kybe
'Twould put me to my slipper: But I feele not
This Deity in my bosome: 'Twentie consciences
That stand 'twixt me, and *Millaine*, candied be they,
And melt ere they mollest: Heere lies your Brother,
No better then the earth he lies vpon,
If he were that which now hee's like (that's dead)
Whom I with this obedient steele (three inches of it)
Can lay to bed for euer: whiles you doing thus,
To the perpetuall winke for aye might put

This ancient morsell: this Sir Prudence, who
Should not vpbraid our course: for all the rest
They'l take suggestion, as a Cat laps milke,
They'l tell the clocke, to any businesse that
We say befits the houre.

   Seb. Thy case, deere Friend
Shall be my president: As thou got'st *Millaine*,
I'le come by *Naples:* Draw thy sword, one stroke
Shall free thee from the tribute which thou paiest,
And I the King shall loue thee.

   Ant. Draw together:
And when I reare my hand, do you the like
To fall it on *Gonzalo*.

   Seb. O, but one word.

            Enter Ariell with Musicke and Song.

   Ariel. My Master through his Art foresees the danger
That you (his friend) are in, and sends me forth
(For else his proiect dies) to keepe them liuing.

              Sings in Gonzaloes eare.

        While you here do snoaring lie,
        Open-ey'd Conspiracie
        His time doth take:
        If of Life you keepe a care,
        Shake off slumber and beware.
        Awake, awake.

   Ant. Then let vs both be sodaine.

   Gon. Now, good Angels preserue the King.

   Alo. Why how now hoa; awake? why are you drawn?
Wherefore this ghastly looking?

   Gon. What's the matter?

   Seb. Whiles we stood here securing your repose,
(Euen now) we heard a hollow burst of bellowing

Like Buls, or rather Lyons, did't not wake you?
It strooke mine eare most terribly.

Alo. I heard nothing.

Ant. O, 'twas a din to fright a Monsters eare;
To make an earthquake: sure it was the roare
Of a whole heard of Lyons.

Alo. Heard you this *Gonzalo*?

Gon. Vpon mine honour, Sir, I heard a humming,
(And that a strange one too) which did awake me:
I shak'd you Sir, and cride: as mine eyes opend,
I saw their weapons drawne: there was a noyse,
That's verily: 'tis best we stand vpon our guard;
Or that we quit this place: let's draw our weapons.

Alo. Lead off this ground & let's make further search
For my poore sonne.

Gon. Heauens keepe him from these Beasts:
For he is sure i'th Island.

Alo. Lead away.

Ariell. Prospero my Lord, shall know what I haue done.
So (King) goe safely on to seeke thy Son.   *Exeunt.*

Scæna Secunda.

Enter Caliban, *with a burthen of Wood*
(*a noyse of Thunder heard.*)

Cal. All the infections that the Sunne suckes vp
From Bogs, Fens, Flats, on *Prosper* fall, and make him
By ynch-meale a disease: his Spirits heare me,
And yet I needes must curse. But they'll nor pinch,
Fright me with Vrchyn-shewes, pitch me i'th mire,
Nor lead me like a fire-brand, in the darke
Out of my way, vnlesse he bid 'em; but
For euery trifle, are they set vpon me,
Sometime like Apes, that moe and chatter at me,
And after bite me: then like Hedg-hogs, which
Lye tumbling in my bare-foote way, and mount
Their pricks at my foot-fall: sometime am I
All wound with Adders, who with clouen tongues
Doe hisse me into madnesse: Lo, now Lo,
                    Enter Trinculo.
Here comes a Spirit of his, and to torment me
For bringing wood in slowly: I'le fall flat,
Perchance he will not minde me.

Tri. Here's neither bush, nor shrub to beare off any
weather at all: and another Storme brewing, I heare it sing
ith' winde: yond same blacke cloud, yond huge one, lookes
like a foule bumbard that would shed his licquor: if it
should thunder, as it did before, I know not where to hide
my head: yond same cloud cannot choose but fall by paile-
fuls. What haue we here, a man, or a fish? dead or aliue? a
fish, hee smels like a fish: a very ancient and fish-like smell:

a kinde of, not of the newest poore-Iohn: a strange fish:
were I in *England* now (as once I was) and had but this fish
painted; not a holiday-foole there but would giue a peece
of siluer: there, would this Monster, make a man: any
strange beast there, makes a man: when they will not giue
a doit to relieue a lame Begger, they will lay out ten to see
a dead *Indian*: Leg'd like a man; and his Finnes like Armes:
warme o' my troth: I doe now let loose my opinion; hold it
no longer; this is no fish, but an Islander, that hath lately
suffered by a Thunderbolt: Alas, the storme is come againe:
my best way is to creepe vnder his Gaberdine: there is no
other shelter hereabout: Misery acquaints a man with
strange bedfellowes: I will here shrowd till the dregges of
the storme be past.

Enter Stephano singing.

Ste. I shall no more to sea, to sea, here shall I dye ashore.
This is a very scuruy tune to sing at a mans
Funerall: well, here's my comfort.

Drinkes.

Sings. *The Master, the Swabber, the Boate-swaine & I;*
The Gunner, and his Mate
Lou'd Mall, Meg, and Marrian, and Margerie,
But none of vs car'd for Kate.
For she had a tongue with a tang,
Would cry to a Sailor goe hang:
She lou'd not the sauour of Tar nor of Pitch,
Yet a Tailor might scratch her where ere she did itch.
Then to Sea Boyes, and let her goe hang.
This is a scuruy tune too:
But here's my comfort.

drinks.

Cal. Doe not torment me: oh.

Ste. What's the matter?

Haue we diuels here?

Doe you put trickes vpon's with Saluages, and Men of *Inde?* ha? I haue not scap'd drowning, to be afeard now of your foure legges: for it hath bin said; as proper a man as euer went on foure legs, cannot make him giue ground: and it shall be said so againe, while *Stephano* breathes at' nostrils.

Cal. The Spirit torments me: oh.

Ste. This is some Monster of the Isle, with foure legs; who hath got (as I take it) an Ague: where the diuell should he learne our language? I will giue him some reliefe if it be but for that: if I can recouer him, and keepe him tame, and get to *Naples* with him, he's a Present for any Emperour that euer trod on Neates-leather.

Cal. Doe not torment me 'prethee: I'le bring my wood home faster.

Ste. He's in his fit now; and doe's not talke after the wisest; hee shall taste of my Bottle: if hee haue neuer drunke wine afore, it will goe neere to remoue his Fit: if I can recouer him, and keepe him tame, I will not take too much for him; hee shall pay for him that hath him, and that soundly.

Cal. Thou do'st me yet but little hurt; thou wilt anon, I know it by thy trembling: Now *Prosper* works vpon thee.

Ste. Come on your wayes: open your mouth: here is that which will giue language to you Cat; open your mouth; this will shake your shaking, I can tell you, and that soundly: you cannot tell who's your friend; open your chaps againe.

Tri. I should know that voyce:

It should be,

But hee is dround; and these are diuels; O defend me.

Ste. Foure legges and two voyces; a most delicate Monster: his forward voyce now is to speake well of his friend; his backward voice, is to vtter foule speeches, and to detract: if all the wine in my bottle will recouer him, I will helpe his Ague: Come: Amen, I will poure some in thy other mouth.

Tri. Stephano.

Ste. Doth thy other mouth call me? Mercy, mercy: This is a diuell, and no Monster: I will leaue him, I haue no long Spoone.

Tri. Stephano: if thou beest *Stephano*, touch me, and speake to me: for I am *Trinculo*; be not afeard, thy good friend *Trinculo*.

Ste. If thou bee'st *Trinculo*: come foorth: I'le pull thee by the lesser legges: if any be *Trinculo's* legges, these are they: Thou art very *Trinculo* indeede: how cam'st thou to be the siege of this Moone-calfe? Can he vent *Trinculo's*?

Tri. I tooke him to be kil'd with a thunder-strok; but art thou not dround *Stephano*: I hope now thou art not dround: Is the Storme ouer-blowne? I hid mee vnder the dead Moone-Calfes Gaberdine, for feare of the Storme: And art thou liuing *Stephano*? O *Stephano*, two *Neapolitanes* scap'd?

Ste. 'Prethee doe not turne me about, my stomacke is not constant.

Cal. These be fine things, and if they be not sprights: that's a braue God, and beares Celestiall liquor: I will kneele to him.

Ste. How did'st thou scape?
How cam'st thou hither?
Sweare by this Bottle how thou cam'st hither: I escap'd vpon a But of Sacke, which the Saylors heaued o'reboord,

by this Bottle which I made of the barke of a Tree, with mine owne hands, since I was cast a'shore.

Cal. I'le sweare vpon that Bottle, to be thy true subiect, for the liquor is not earthly.

St. Heere: sweare then how thou escap'dst.

Tri. Swom ashore (man) like a Ducke: I can swim like a Ducke i'le be sworne.

Ste. Here, kisse the Booke.
Though thou canst swim like a Ducke, thou art made like a Goose.

Tri. O *Stephano*, ha'st any more of this?

Ste. The whole But (man) my Cellar is in a rocke by th'sea-side, where my Wine is hid:
How now Moone-Calfe, how do's thine Ague?

Cal. Ha'st thou not dropt from heauen?

Ste. Out o'th Moone I doe assure thee. I was the Man ith' Moone, when time was.

Cal. I haue seene thee in her: and I doe adore thee: My Mistris shew'd me thee, and thy Dog, and thy Bush.

Ste. Come, sweare to that: kisse the Booke: I will furnish it anon with new Contents: Sweare.

Tri. By this good light, this is a very shallow Monster: I afeard of him? a very weake Monster:
The Man ith' Moone?
A most poore creadulous Monster:
Well drawne Monster, in good sooth.

Cal. Ile shew thee euery fertill ynch 'oth Island: and I will kisse thy foote: I prethee be my god.

Tri. By this light, a most perfidious, and drunken Monster, when's god's a sleepe he'll rob his Bottle.

Cal. Ile kisse thy foot. Ile sweare my selfe thy Subiect.

Ste. Come on then: downe and sweare.

Tri. I shall laugh my selfe to death at this puppi-headed Monster: a most scuruie Monster: I could finde in my heart to beate him.

Ste. Come, kisse.

Tri. But that the poore Monster's in drinke:
An abhominable Monster.

Cal. I'le shew thee the best Springs: I'le plucke thee Berries: I'le fish for thee; and get thee wood enough.
A plague vpon the Tyrant that I serue;
I'le beare him no more Stickes, but follow thee, thou won-drous man.

Tri. A most rediculous Monster, to make a wonder of a poore drunkard.

Cal. I 'prethee let me bring thee where Crabs grow; and I with my long nayles will digge thee pig-nuts; show thee a Iayes nest, and instruct thee how to snare the nimble Marmazet: I'le bring thee to clustering Philbirts, and some-times I'le get thee young Scamels from the Rocke: Wilt thou goe with me?

Ste. I pre'thee now lead the way without any more talk-ing. *Trinculo*, the King, and all our company else being dround, wee will inherit here: Here; beare my Bottle: Fel-low *Trinculo*; we'll fill him by and by againe.

Caliban Sings drunkenly.

Farewell Master; farewell, farewell.

Tri. A howling Monster: a drunken Monster.

> *Cal. No more dams I'le make for fish,*
> *Nor fetch in firing, at requiring,*
> *Nor scrape trenchering, nor wash dish,*
> *Ban' ban' Cacalyban*
> *Has a new Master, get a new Man.*

Freedome, high-day, high-day freedome, freedome high-day, freedome.

 Ste. O braue Monster; lead the way.   *Exeunt.*

Actus Tertius. Scœna Prima.

Enter Ferdinand (bearing a Log.)

Fer. There be some Sports are painfull; & their labor
Delight in them set off: Some kindes of basenesse
Are nobly vndergon; and most poore matters
Point to rich ends: this my meane Taske
Would be as heauy to me, as odious, but
The Mistris which I serue, quickens what's dead,
And makes my labours, pleasures: O She is
Ten times more gentle, then her Father's crabbed;
And he's compos'd of harshnesse. I must remoue
Some thousands of these Logs, and pile them vp,
Vpon a sore iniunction; my sweet Mistris
Weepes when she sees me worke, & saies, such basenes
Had neuer like Executor: I forget:
But these sweet thoughts, doe euen refresh my labours,
Most busie lest, when I doe it.

Enter Miranda and Prospero.

Mir. Alas, now pray you
Worke not so hard: I would the lightning had
Burnt vp those Logs that you are enioynd to pile:
Pray set it downe, and rest you: when this burnes
'Twill weepe for hauing wearied you: my Father
Is hard at study; pray now rest your selfe,
Hee's safe for these three houres.

Fer. O most deere Mistris,
The Sun will set before I shall discharge
What I must striue to do.

Mir. If you'l sit downe

Ile beare your Logges the while: pray giue me that,
Ile carry it to the pile.

Fer. No precious Creature,
I had rather cracke my sinewes, breake my backe,
Then you should such dishonor vndergoe,
While I sit lazy by.

Mir. It would become me
As well as it do's you; and I should do it
With much more ease: for my good will is to it,
And yours it is against.

Pro. Poore worme thou art infected,
This visitation shewes it.

Mir. You looke wearily.

Fer. No, noble Mistris, 'tis fresh morning with me
When you are by at night: I do beseech you
Cheefely, that I might set it in my prayers,
What is your name?

Mir. Miranda, O my Father,
I haue broke your hest to say so.

Fer. Admir'd *Miranda*,
Indeede the top of Admiration, worth
What's deerest to the world: full many a Lady
I haue ey'd with best regard, and many a time
Th'harmony of their tongues, hath into bondage
Brought my too diligent eare: for seuerall vertues
Haue I lik'd seuerall women, neuer any
VVith so full soule, but some defect in her
Did quarrell with the noblest grace she ow'd,
And put it to the foile. But you, O you,
So perfect, and so peetlesse, are created
Of euerie Creatures best.

Mir. I do not know

One of my sexe; no womans face remember,
Saue from my glasse, mine owne: Nor haue I seene
More that I may call men, then you good friend,
And my deere Father: how features are abroad
I am skillesse of; but by my modestie
(The iewell in my dower) I would not wish
Any Companion in the world but you:
Nor can imagination forme a shape
Besides your selfe, to like of: but I prattle
Something too wildely, and my Fathers precepts
I therein do forget.

   Fer. I am, in my condition
A Prince (*Miranda*) I do thinke a King
(I would not so) and would no more endure
This wodden slauerie, then to suffer
The flesh-flie blow my mouth: heare my soule speake.
The verie instant that I saw you, did
My heart flie to your seruice, there resides
To make me slaue to it, and for your sake
Am I this patient Logge-man.

   Mir. Do you loue me?

   Fer. O heauen; O earth, beare witnes to this sound,
And crowne what I professe with kinde euent
If I speake true: if hollowly, inuert
VVhat best is boaded me, to mischiefe: I,
Beyond all limit of what else i'th world
Do loue, prize, honor you.

   Mir. I am a foole
To weepe at what I am glad of.

   Pro. Faire encounter
Of two most rare affections: heauens raine grace
On that which breeds betweene 'em.

Fer. VVherefore weepe you?

Mir. At mine vnworthinesse, that dare not offer
VVhat I desire to giue; and much lesse take
VVhat I shall die to want: But this is trifling,
And all the more it seekes to hide it selfe,
The bigger bulke it shewes. Hence bashfull cunning,
And prompt me plaine and holy innocence.
I am your wife, if you will marrie me;
If not, Ile die your maid: to be your fellow
You may denie me, but Ile be your seruant
VVhether you will or no.

Fer. My Mistris (deerest)
And I thus humble euer.

Mir. My husband then?

Fer. I, with a heart as willing
As bondage ere of freedome: heere's my hand.

Mir. And mine, with my heart in't; and now farewel
Till halfe an houre hence.

Fer. A thousand, thousand.   *Exeunt.*

Pro. So glad of this as they I cannot be,
VVho are surpriz'd with all; but my reioycing
At nothing can be more: Ile to my booke,
For yet ere supper time, must I performe
Much businesse appertaining.   *Exit.*

Scœna Secunda.

Enter Caliban, Stephano, and Trinculo.

Ste. Tell not me, when the But is out we will drinke water, not a drop before; therefore beare vp, & boord em' Seruant Monster, drinke to me.

Trin. Seruant Monster? the folly of this Iland, they say there's but fiue vpon this Isle; we are three of them, if th'other two be brain'd like vs, the State totters.

Ste. Drinke seruant Monster when I bid thee, thy eies are almost set in thy head.

Trin. VVhere should they bee set else? hee were a braue Monster indeede if they were set in his taile.

Ste. My man-Monster hath drown'd his tongue in sacke: for my part the Sea cannot drowne mee, I swam ere I could recouer the shore, fiue and thirtie Leagues off and on, by this light thou shalt bee my Lieutenant Monster, or my Standard.

Trin. Your Lieutenant if you list, hee's no standard.

Ste. VVeel not run Monsieur Monster.

Trin. Nor go neither: but you'l lie like dogs, and yet say nothing neither.

Ste. Moone-calfe, speak once in thy life, if thou beest a good Moone-calfe.

Cal. How does thy honour? Let me licke thy shooe: Ile not serue him, he is not valiant.

Trin. Thou liest most ignorant Monster, I am in case to iustle a Constable: why, thou debosh'd Fish thou, was there euer man a Coward, that hath drunk so much Sacke as I

to day? wilt thou tell a monstrous lie, being but halfe a
Fish, and halfe a Monster?

Cal. Loe, how he mockes me, wilt thou let him my Lord?

Trin. Lord, quoth he? that a Monster should be such a
Naturall?

Cal. Loe, loe againe: bite him to death I prethee.

Ste. Trinculo, keepe a good tongue in your head: If you
proue a mutineere, the next Tree: the poore Monster's my
subiect, and he shall not suffer indignity.

Cal. I thanke my noble Lord. Wilt thou be pleas'd to
hearken once againe to the suite I made to thee?

Ste. Marry will I: kneele, and repeate it,
I will stand, and so shall *Trinculo*.

Enter Ariell inuisible.

Cal. As I told thee before, I am subiect to a Tirant,
A Sorcerer, that by his cunning hath cheated me
Of the Island.

Ariell. Thou lyest.

Cal. Thou lyest, thou iesting Monkey thou:
I would my valiant Master would destroy thee.
I do not lye.

Ste. Trinculo, if you trouble him any more in's tale,
By this hand, I will supplant some of your teeth.

Trin. Why, I said nothing.

Ste. Mum then, and no more: proceed.

Cal. I say by Sorcery he got this Isle
From me, he got it. If thy Greatnesse will
Reuenge it on him, (for I know thou dar'st)
But this Thing dare not.

Ste. That's most certaine.

Cal. Thou shalt be Lord of it, and Ile serue thee.

Ste. How now shall this be compast?
Canst thou bring me to the party?

Cal. Yea, yea my Lord, Ile yeeld him thee asleepe,
Where thou maist knocke a naile into his head.

Ariell. Thou liest, thou canst not.

Cal. What a py'de Ninnie's this? Thou scuruy patch:
I do beseech thy Greatnesse giue him blowes,
And take his bottle from him: When that's gone,
He shall drinke nought but brine, for Ile not shew him
Where the quicke Freshes are.

Ste. *Trinculo*, run into no further danger:
Interrupt the Monster one word further, and by this hand,
Ile turne my mercie out o'doores, and make a Stockfish of
thee.

Trin. Why, what did I? I did nothing:
Ile go farther off.

Ste. Didst thou not say he lyed?

Ariell. Thou liest.

Ste. Do I so? Take thou that,
As you like this, giue me the lye another time.

Trin. I did not giue the lie: Out o'your wittes, and hearing too?
A pox o'your bottle, this can Sacke and drinking doo: A
murren on your Monster, and the diuell take your fingers.

Cal. Ha, ha, ha.

Ste. Now forward with your Tale: prethee stand further off.

Cal. Beate him enough: after a little time
Ile beate him too.

Ste. Stand farther: Come proceede.

Cal. Why, as I told thee, 'tis a custome with him
I'th afternoone to sleepe: there thou maist braine him,
Hauing first seiz'd his bookes: Or with a logge

Batter his skull, or paunch him with a stake,
Or cut his wezand with thy knife. Remember
First to possesse his Bookes; for without them
Hee's but a Sot, as I am; nor hath not
One Spirit to command: they all do hate him
As rootedly as I. Burne but his Bookes,
He ha's braue Vtensils (for so he calles them)
Which when he ha's a house, hee'l decke withall.
And that most deeply to consider, is
The beautie of his daughter: he himselfe
Cals her a non-pareill: I neuer saw a woman
But onely *Sycorax* my Dam, and she;
But she as farre surpasseth *Sycorax*,
As great'st do's least.

   Ste. Is it so braue a Lasse?

   Cal. I Lord, she will become thy bed, I warrant,
And bring thee forth braue brood.

   Ste. Monster, I will kill this man: his daughter and I will
be King and Queene, saue our Graces: and *Trinculo* and thy
selfe shall be Vice-royes:
Dost thou like the plot *Trinculo?*

   Trin. Excellent.

   Ste. Giue me thy hand, I am sorry I beate thee:
But while thou liu'st keepe a good tongue in thy head.

   Cal. Within this halfe houre will he be asleepe,
Wilt thou destroy him then?

   Ste. I on mine honour.

   Ariell. This will I tell my Master.

   Cal. Thou mak'st me merry: I am full of pleasure,
Let vs be iocond. Will you troule the Catch
You taught me but whileare?

   Ste. At thy request Monster, I will do reason,

Any reason: Come on *Trinculo*, let vs sing.

Sings.

> *Flout'em, and cout'em: and skowt'em, and flout'em,*
> *Thought is free.*

Cal. That's not the tune.

Ariell plaies the tune on a Tabor and Pipe.

Ste. What is this same?

Trin. This is the tune of our Catch, plaid by the picture of No-body.

Ste. If thou beest a man, shew thy selfe in thy likenes: If thou beest a diuell, take't as thou list.

Trin. O forgiue me my sinnes.

Ste. He that dies payes all debts: I defie thee; Mercy vpon vs.

Cal. Art thou affeard?

Ste. No Monster, not I.

Cal. Be not affeard, the Isle is full of noyses,
Sounds, and sweet aires, that giue delight and hurt not:
Sometimes a thousand twangling Instruments
Will hum about mine eares; and sometime voices,
That if I then had wak'd after long sleepe,
Will make me sleepe againe, and then in dreaming,
The clouds methought would open, and shew riches
Ready to drop vpon me, that when I wak'd
I cri'de to dreame againe.

Ste. This will proue a braue kingdome to me,
Where I shall haue my Musicke for nothing.

Cal. When *Prospero* is destroy'd.

Ste. That shall be by and by:
I remember the storie.

Trin. The sound is going away,
Lets follow it, and after do our worke.

Ste. Leade Monster,
Wee'l follow: I would I could see this Taborer,
He layes it on.
  Trin. Wilt come?
Ile follow *Stephano*.   *Exeunt.*

Scena Tertia.

Enter Alonso, Sebastian, Anthonio, Gonzallo,
Adrian, Francisco, &c.

Gon. By'r lakin, I can goe no further, Sir,
My old bones akes: here's a maze trod indeede
Through fourth-rights, & Meanders: by your patience,
I needes must rest me.

Al. Old Lord, I cannot blame thee,
Who, am my selfe attach'd with wearinesse
To th'dulling of my spirits: Sit downe, and rest:
Euen here I will put off my hope, and keepe it
No longer for my Flatterer: he is droun'd
Whom thus we stray to finde, and the Sea mocks
Our frustrate search on land: well, let him goe.

Ant. I am right glad, that he's so out of hope:
Doe not for one repulse forgoe the purpose
That you resolu'd t'effect.

Seb. The next aduantage will we take throughly.

Ant. Let it be to night,
For now they are oppress'd with trauaile, they
Will not, nor cannot vse such vigilance
As when they are fresh.

Solemne and strange Musicke: and Prosper on the top (inuisible:)
Enter seuerall strange shapes, bringing in a Banket; and dance
about it with gentle actions of salutations, and inuiting
the King, &c. to eate, they depart.

Seb. I say to night: no more.

Al. What harmony is this? my good friends, harke.

Gon. Maruellous sweet Musicke.

Alo. Giue vs kind keepers, heauẽs: what were these?

Seb. A liuing *Drolerie:* now I will beleeue
That there are Vnicornes: that in *Arabia*
There is one Tree, the Phœnix throne, one Phœnix
At this houre reigning there.

Ant. Ile beleeue both:
And what do's else want credit, come to me
And Ile besworne 'tis true: Trauellers nere did lye,
Though fooles at home condemne 'em.

Gon. If in *Naples*
I should report this now, would they beleeue me?
If I should say I saw such Islands;
(For certes, these are people of the Island)
Who though they are of monstrous shape, yet note
Their manners are more gentle, kinde, then of
Our humaine generation you shall finde
Many, nay almost any.

Pro. Honest Lord,
Thou hast said well: for some of you there present;
Are worse then diuels.

Al. I cannot too much muse
Such shapes, such gesture, and such sound expressing
(Although they want the vse of tongue) a kinde
Of excellent dumbe discourse.

Pro. Praise in departing.

Fr. They vanish'd strangely.

Seb. No matter, since
They haue left their Viands behinde; for wee haue stomacks.
Wilt please you taste of what is here?

Alo. Not I.

Gon. Faith Sir, you neede not feare: when wee were Boyes
Who would beleeue that there were Mountayneeres,

Dew-lapt, like Buls, whose throats had hanging at 'em
Wallets of flesh? or that there were such men
Whose heads stood in their brests? which now we finde
Each putter out of fiue for one, will bring vs
Good warrant of.

 Al. I will stand to, and feede,
Although my last, no matter, since I feele
The best is past: brother: my Lord, the Duke,
Stand too, and doe as we.

 Thunder and Lightning. Enter Ariell (like a Harpey) claps his wings
  vpon the Table, and with a quient deuice the Banquet vanishes.

 Ar. You are three men of sinne, whom destiny
That hath to instrument this lower world,
And what is in't: the neuer surfeited Sea,
Hath caus'd to belch vp you; and on this Island,
Where man doth not inhabit, you 'mongst men,
Being most vnfit to liue: I haue made you mad;
And euen with such like valour, men hang, and drowne
Their proper selues: you fooles, I and my fellowes
Are ministers of Fate, the Elements
Of whom your swords are temper'd, may as well
Wound the loud windes, or with bemockt-at-Stabs
Kill the still closing waters, as diminish
One dowle that's in my plumbe: My fellow ministers
Are like-invulnerable: if you could hurt,
Your swords are now too massie for your strengths,
And will not be vplifted: But remember
(For that's my businesse to you) that you three
From *Millaine* did supplant good *Prospero*,
Expos'd vnto the Sea (which hath requit it)
Him, and his innocent childe: for which foule deed,
The Powres, delaying (not forgetting) haue

Incens'd the Seas, and Shores; yea, all the Creatures
Against your peace: Thee of thy Sonne, *Alonso*
They haue bereft; and doe pronounce by me
Lingring perdition (worse then any death
Can be at once) shall step, by step attend
You, and your wayes, whose wraths to guard you from,
Which here, in this most desolate Isle, else fals
Vpon your heads, is nothing but hearts-sorrow,
And a cleere life ensuing.

> *He vanishes in Thunder: then (to soft Musicke.) Enter*
> *the shapes againe, and daunce (with mockes and mowes)*
> *and carrying out the Table.*

Pro. Brauely the figure of this *Harpie*, hast thou
Perform'd (my *Ariell*) a grace it had deuouring:
Of my Instruction, hast thou nothing bated
In what thou had'st to say: so with good life,
And obseruation strange, my meaner ministers
Their seuerall kindes haue done: my high charmes work,
And these (mine enemies) are all knit vp
In their distractions: they now are in my powre;
And in these fits, I leaue them, while I visit
Yong *Ferdinand* (whom they suppose is droun'd)
And his, and mine lou'd darling.

Gon. I'th name of something holy, Sir, why stand you
In this strange stare?

Al. O, it is monstrous: monstrous:
Me thought the billowes spoke, and told me of it,
The windes did sing it to me: and the Thunder
(That deepe and dreadfull Organ-Pipe) pronounc'd
The name of *Prosper*: it did base my Trespasse,
Therefore my Sonne i'th Ooze is bedded; and
I'le seeke him deeper then ere plummet sounded,

And with him there lye mudded. *Exit.*

    Seb. But one feend at a time,
Ile fight their Legions ore.

    Ant. Ile be thy Second. *Exeunt.*

    Gon. All three of them are desperate: their great guilt
(Like poyson giuen to worke a great time after)
Now gins to bite the spirits: I doe beseech you
(That are of suppler ioynts) follow them swiftly,
And hinder them from what this extasie
May now prouoke them to.

    Ad. Follow, I pray you. *Exeunt omnes.*

Actus Quartus. Scena Prima.

Enter Prospero, Ferdinand, and Miranda.

Pro. If I haue too austerely punish'd you,
Your compensation makes amends, for I
Haue giuen you here, a third of mine owne life,
Or that for which I liue: who, once againe
I tender to thy hand: All thy vexations
Were but my trials of thy loue, and thou
Hast strangely stood the test: here, afore heauen
I ratifie this my rich guift: O *Ferdinand*,
Doe not smile at me, that I boast her of,
For thou shalt finde she will out-strip all praise
And make it halt, behinde her.

Fer. I doe beleeue it
Against an Oracle.

Pro. Then, as my guest, and thine owne acquisition
Worthily purchas'd, take my daughter: But
If thou do'st breake her Virgin-knot, before
All sanctimonious ceremonies may
With full and holy right, be ministred,
No sweet aspersion shall the heauens let fall
To make this contract grow; but barraine hate,
Sower-ey'd disdaine, and discord shall bestrew
The vnion of your bed, with weedes so loathly
That you shall hate it both: Therefore take heede,
As Hymens Lamps shall light you.

Fer. As I hope
For quiet dayes, faire Issue, and long life,
With such loue, as 'tis now the murkiest den,

57

The most opportune place, the strongst suggestion,
Our worser *Genius* can, shall neuer melt
Mine honor into lust, to take away
The edge of that dayes celebration,
When I shall thinke, or *Phœbus* Steeds are founderd,
Or Night kept chain'd below.

  Pro. Fairely spoke;
Sit then, and talke with her, she is thine owne;
What *Ariell*; my industrious seruāt *Ariell*.

            Enter Ariell.

  Ar. What would my potent master? here I am.

  Pro. Thou, and thy meaner fellowes, your last seruice
Did worthily performe: and I must vse you
In such another tricke: goe bring the rabble
(Ore whom I giue thee powre) here, to this place:
Incite them to quicke motion, for I must
Bestow vpon the eyes of this yong couple
Some vanity of mine Art: it is my promise,
And they expect it from me.

  Ar. Presently?

  Pro. I: with a twincke.

  Ar. Before you can say come, and goe,
And breathe twice; and cry, so, so:
Each one tripping on his Toe,
Will be here with mop, and mowe.
Doe you loue me Master? no?

  Pro. Dearely, my delicate *Ariell*: doe not approach
Till thou do'st heare me call.

  Ar. Well: I conceiue.   *Exit.*

  Pro. Looke thou be true: doe not giue dalliance
Too much the raigne: the strongest oathes, are straw
To th'fire ith' blood: be more abstenious,

Or else good night your vow.

   Fer. I warrant you, Sir,
The white cold virgin Snow, vpon my heart
Abates the ardour of my Liuer.

   Pro. Well.
Now come my *Ariell*, bring a Corolary,
Rather then want a Spirit; appear, & pertly.
                 Soft musick.
No tongue: all eyes: be silent.
                 Enter Iris.

   Ir. Ceres, most bounteous Lady, thy rich Leas
Of Wheate, Rye, Barley, Fetches, Oates and Pease;
Thy Turphie-Mountaines, where liue nibling Sheepe,
And flat Medes thetchd with Stouer, them to keepe:
Thy bankes with pioned, and twilled brims
Which spungie *Aprill*, at thy hest betrims;
To make cold Nymphes chast crownes; & thy broome-
   groues;
Whose shadow the dismissed Batchelor loues,
Being lasse-lorne: thy pole-clipt vineyard,
And thy Sea-marge stirrile, and rockey-hard,
Where thou thy selfe do'st ayre, the Queene o'th Skie,
Whose watry Arch, and messenger, am I.
Bids thee leaue these, & with her soueraigne grace,
                Iuno descends.
Here on this grasse-plot, in this very place
To come, and sport: here Peacocks flye amaine:
Approach, rich *Ceres*, her to entertaine.
                Enter Ceres.

   Cer. Haile, many-coloured Messenger, that nere
Do'st disobey the wife of *Iupiter:*
Who, with thy saffron wings, vpon my flowres

Diffusest hony drops, refreshing showres,
And with each end of thy blew bowe do'st crowne
My boskie acres, and my vnshrubd downe,
Rich scarph to my proud earth: why hath thy Queene
Summond me hither, to this short gras'd Greene?

   Ir. A contract of true Loue, to celebrate,
And some donation freely to estate
On the bles'd Louers.

   Cer. Tell me heauenly Bowe,
If *Venus* or her Sonne, as thou do'st know,
Doe now attend the Queene? since they did plot
The meanes, that duskie *Dis*, my daughter got,
Her, and her blind-Boyes scandald company,
I haue forsworne.

   Ir. Of her societie
Be not afraid: I met her deitie
Cutting the clouds towards *Paphos*: and her Son
Doue-drawn with her: here thought they to haue done
Some wanton charme, vpon this Man and Maide,
Whose vowes are, that no bed-right shall be paid
Till *Hymens* Torch be lighted: but in vaine,
Marses hot Minion is returnd againe,
Her waspish headed sonne, has broke his arrowes,
Swears he will shoote no more, but play with Sparrows,
And be a Boy right out.

   Cer. Highest Queene of State,
Great *Iuno* comes, I know her by her gate.

   Iu. How do's my bounteous sister? goe with me
To blesse this twaine, that they may prosperous be,
And honourd in their Issue.

They Sing.
Iu. Honor, riches, marriage, blessing,
Long continuance, and encreasing,
Hourely ioyes, be still vpon you,
Iuno sings her blessings on you.
Earths increase, foyzon plentie,
Barnes, and Garners, neuer empty.
Vines, with clustring bunches growing,
Plants, wtth goodly burthen bowing:
Spring come to you at the farthest,
In the very end of Haruest.
Scarcity and want shall shun you,
Ceres *blessing so is on you.*

Fer. This is a most maiesticke vision, and
Harmonious charmingly: may I be bold
To thinke these spirits?

Pro. Spirits, which by mine Art
I haue from their confines call'd to enact
My present fancies.

Fer. Let me liue here euer,
So rare a wondred Father, and a wife
Makes this place Paradise.

Pro. Sweet now, silence:
Iuno and *Ceres* whisper seriously,
There's something else to doe: hush, and be mute
Or else our spell is mar'd.

Iuno *and* Ceres *whisper, and send* Iris *on employment.*

Iris. You Nimphs cald *Nayades* of ye windring brooks,
With your sedg'd crownes, and euer-harmelesse lookes,
Leaue your crispe channels, and on this green-Land
Answere your summons, *Iuno* do's command.

Come temperate *Nimphes*, and helpe to celebrate
A Contract of true Loue: be not too late.

Enter Certaine Nimphes.

You Sun-burn'd Sicklemen of August weary,
Come hether from the furrow, and be merry,
Make holly day: your Rye-straw hats put on,
And these fresh Nimphes encounter euery one
In Country footing.

*Enter certaine Reapers (properly habited:) they ioyne with the
Nimphes, in a gracefull dance, towards the end whereof,* Prospero
*starts sodainly and speakes, after which to a strange hollow
and confused noyse, they heauily vanish.*

Pro. I had forgot that foule conspiracy
Of the beast *Calliban*, and his confederates
Against my life: the minute of their plot
Is almost come: Well done, auoid: no more.

Fer. This is strange: your fathers in some passion
That workes him strongly.

Mir. Neuer till this day
Saw I him touch'd with anger, so distemper'd.

Pro. You doe looke (my son) in a mou'd sort,
As if you were dismaid: be cheerefull Sir,
Our Reuels now are ended: These our actors,
(As I foretold you) were all Spirits, and
Are melted into Ayre, into thin Ayre,
And like the baselesse fabricke of this vision
The Clowd-capt Towres, the gorgeous Pallaces,
The solemne Temples, the great Globe it selfe,
Yea, all which it inherit, shall dissolue,
And like this insubstantiall Pageant faded
Leaue not a racke behinde: we are such stuffe
As dreames are made on; and our little life

Is rounded with a sleepe: Sir, I am vext,
Beare with my weakenesse, my old braine is troubled:
Be not disturb'd with my infirmitie,
If you be pleas'd, retire into my Cell,
And there repose, a turne or two, Ile walke
To still my beating minde.

    Fer. Mir. We wish your peace.   *Exit.*

    Pro. Come with a thought; I thank thee *Ariell*: come.
                Enter Ariell.

    Ar. Thy thoughts I cleaue to, what's thy pleasure?
    Pro. Spirit: We must prepare to meet with *Caliban*.

    Ar. I my Commander, when I presented *Ceres*
I thought to haue told thee of it, but I fear'd
Least I might anger thee.

    Pro. Say again, where didst thou leaue these varlots?

    Ar. I told you Sir, they were red-hot with drinking,
So full of valour, that they smote the ayre
For breathing in their faces: beate the ground
For kissing of their feete; yet alwaies bending
Towards their proiect: then I beate my Tabor,
At which like vnback't colts they prickt their eares,
Aduanc'd their eye-lids, lifted vp their noses
As they smelt musicke, so I charm'd their eares
That Calfe-like, they my lowing follow'd, through
Tooth'd briars, sharpe firzes, pricking gosse, & thorns,
Which entred their fraile shins: at last I left them
I'th' filthy mantled poole beyond your Cell,
There dancing vp to th'chins, that the fowle Lake
Ore-stunck their feet.

    Pro. This was well done (my bird)
Thy shape inuisible retaine thou still:
The trumpery in my house, goe bring it hither

For stale to catch these theeues.

 Ar. I go, I goe.   *Exit.*

 Pro. A Deuill, a borne-Deuill, on whose nature
Nurture can neuer sticke: on whom my paines
Humanely taken, all, all lost, quite lost,
And, as with age, his body ouglier growes,
So his minde cankers: I will plague them all,
Euen to roaring: Come, hang on them this line.

  Enter Ariell, *loaden with glistering apparell, &c. Enter*
   Caliban, Stephano, *and* Trinculo, *all wet*.

 Cal. Pray you tread softly, that the blinde Mole may not
heare a foot fall: we now are neere his Cell.

 St. Monster, your Fairy, w^c you say is a harmles Fairy,
Has done little better then plaid the Iacke with vs.

 Trin. Monster, I do smell all horse-pisse, at which
My nose is in great indignation.

 Ste. So is mine. Do you heare Monster: If I should
Take a displeasure against you: Looke you.

 Trin. Thou wert but a lost Monster.

 Cal. Good my Lord, giue me thy fauour stil,
Be patient, for the prize Ile bring thee too
Shall hudwinke this mischance: therefore speake softly,
All's husht as midnight yet.

 Trin. I, but to loose our bottles in the Poole.

 Ste. There is not onely disgrace and dishonor in that
Monster, but an infinite losse.

 Tr. That's more to me then my wetting:
Yet this is your harmlesse Fairy, Monster.

 Ste. I will fetch off my bottle,
Though I be o're eares for my labour.

 Cal. Pre-thee (my King) be quiet. Seest thou heere
This is the mouth o'th Cell: no noise, and enter:

Do that good mischeefe, which may make this Island
Thine owne for euer, and I thy *Caliban*
For aye thy foot-licker.

    Ste. Giue me thy hand,
I do begin to haue bloody thoughts.

    Trin. O King *Stephano*, O Peere: O worthy *Stephano*,
Looke what a wardrobe heere is for thee.

    Cal. Let it alone thou foole, it is but trash.

    Tri. Oh, ho, Monster: wee know what belongs to a frip-
pery, O King *Stephano*.

    Ste. Put off that gowne (*Trinculo*) by this hand Ile haue
that gowne.

    Tri. Thy grace shall haue it.

    Cal. The dropsie drowne this foole, what doe you meane
To doate thus on such luggage? let's alone
And doe the murther first: if he awake,
From toe to crowne hee'l fill our skins with pinches,
Make vs strange stuffe.

    Ste. Be you quiet (Monster) Mistris line, is not this my
Ierkin? now is the Ierkin vnder the line: now Ierkin you are
like to lose your haire, & proue a bald Ierkin.

    Trin. Doe, doe; we steale by lyne and leuell, and't like
your grace.

    Ste. I thank thee for that iest; heer's a garment for't: Wit
shall not goe vn-rewarded while I am King of this Country:
Steale by line and leuell, is an excellent passe of pate:
there's another garment for't.

    Tri. Monster, come put some Lime vpon your fingers,
and away with the rest.

    Cal. I will haue none on't: we shall loose our time,
And all be turn'd to Barnacles, or to Apes
With foreheads villanous low.

Ste. Monster, lay to your fingers: helpe to beare this away, where my hogshead of wine is, or Ile turne you out of my kingdome: goe to, carry this.

Tri. And this.

Ste. I, and this.

> *A noyse of Hunters heard. Enter diuers Spirits in shape*
> *of Dogs and Hounds, hunting them about: Prospero and*
> *Ariel setting them on.*

Pro. Hey *Mountaine*, hey.

Ari. Siluer: there it goes, *Siluer*.

Pro. Fury, Fury: there Tyrant, there: harke, harke.
Goe, charge my Goblins that they grinde their ioynts
With dry Convultions, shorten vp their sinewes
With aged Cramps, & more pinch-spotted make them,
Then Pard, or Cat o' Mountaine.

Ari. Harke, they rore.

Pro. Let them be hunted soundly: At this houre
Lies at my mercy all mine enemies:
Shortly shall all my labours end, and thou
Shalt haue the ayre at freedome: for a little
Follow, and doe me seruice.   *Exeunt.*

Actus quintus: Scæna Prima.

     Enter Prospero (*in his Magicke robes*) *and* Ariel.
   Pro. Now do's my Proiect gather to a head:
My charmes cracke not: my Spirits obey, and Time
Goes vpright with his carriage: how's the day?
   Ar. On the sixt hower, at which time, my Lord
You said our worke should cease.
   Pro. I did say so,
When first I rais'd the Tempest: say my Spirit,
How fares the King, and's followers?
   Ar. Confin'd together
In the same fashion, as you gaue in charge,
Iust as you left them; all prisoners Sir
In the *Line-groue* which weather-fends your Cell,
They cannot boudge till your release: The King,
His Brother, and yours, abide all three distracted,
And the remainder mourning ouer them,
Brim full of sorrow, and dismay: but chiefly
Him that you term'd Sir, the good old Lord *Gonzallo*,
His teares runs downe his beard like winters drops
From eaues of reeds: your charm so strongly works 'em
That if you now beheld them, your affections
Would become tender.
   Pro. Dost thou thinke so, Spirit?
   Ar. Mine would, Sir, were I humane.
   Pro. And mine shall.
Hast thou (which art but aire) a touch, a feeling
Of their afflictions, and shall not my selfe,
One of their kinde, that rellish all as sharpely,

Passion as they, be kindlier mou'd then thou art?
Thogh with their high wrongs I am strook to th'quick,
Yet, with my nobler reason, gainst my furie
Doe I take part: the rarer Action is
In vertue, then in vengeance: they, being penitent,
The sole drift of my purpose doth extend
Not a frowne further: Goe, release them *Ariell*,
My Charmes Ile breake, their sences Ile restore,
And they shall be themselues.

   Ar. Ile fetch them, Sir.   *Exit.*

   Pro. Ye Elues of hils, brooks, stãding lakes & groues,
And ye, that on the sands with printlesse foote
Doe chase the ebbing-*Neptune*, and doe flie him
When he comes backe: you demy-Puppets, that
By Moone-shine doe the greene sowre Ringlets make,
Whereof the Ewe not bites: and you, whose pastime
Is to make midnight-Mushrumps, that reioyce
To heare the solemne Curfewe, by whose ayde
(Weake Masters though ye be) I haue bedymn'd
The Noone-tide Sun, call'd forth the mutenous windes,
And twixt the greene Sea, and the azur'd vault
Set roaring warre: To the dread ratling Thunder
Haue I giuen fire, and rifted *Ioues* stowt Oke
With his owne Bolt: The strong bass'd promontorie
Haue I made shake, and by the spurs pluckt vp
The Pyne, and Cedar. Graues at my command
Haue wak'd their sleepers, op'd, and let 'em forth
By my so potent Art. But this rough Magicke
I heere abiure: and when I haue requir'd
Some heauenly Musicke (which euen now I do)
To worke mine end vpon their Sences, that
This Ayrie-charme is for, I'le breake my staffe,

Bury it certaine fadomes in the earth,
And deeper then did euer Plummet sound
Ile drowne my booke.

Solemne musicke.

Heere enters Ariel *before*: *Then* Alonso *with a franticke gesture,*
attended by Gonzalo. Sebastian *and* Anthonio *in like manner*
attended by Adrian *and* Francisco: *They all enter the circle*
which Prospero *had made, and there stand charm'd:*
which Prospero *obseruing, speakes.*

A solemne Ayre, and the best comforter,
To an vnsetled fancie, Cure thy braines
(Now vselesse) boile within thy skull: there stand
For you are Spell-stopt.
Holy *Gonzallo*, Honourable man,
Mine eyes ev'n sociable to the shew of thine
Fall fellowly drops: The charme dissolues apace,
And as the morning steales vpon the night
(Melting the darkenesse) so their rising sences
Begin to chace the ignorant fumes that mantle
Their cleerer reason. O good *Gonzallo*
My true preseruer, and a loyall Sir,
To him thou follow'st; I will pay thy graces
Home both in word, and deede: Most cruelly
Did thou *Alonso*, vse me, and my daughter:
Thy brother was a furtherer in the Act,
Thou art pinch'd for't now *Sebastian*. Flesh, and bloud,
You, brother mine, that entertaine ambition,
Expelld remorse, and nature, whom, with *Sebastian*
(Whose inward pinches therefore are most strong)
Would heere haue kill'd your King: I do forgiue thee,
Vnnaturall though thou art: Their vnderstanding
Begins to swell, and the approching tide

Will shortly fill the reasonable shore
That now ly foule, and muddy: not one of them
That yet lookes on me, or would know me: *Ariell*,
Fetch me the Hat, and Rapier in my Cell,
I will discase me, and my selfe present
As I was sometime *Millaine*: quickly Spirit,
Thou shalt ere long be free.

> *Ariell sings, and helps to attire him.*
> *Where the Bee sucks, there suck I,*
> *In a Cowslips bell, I lie,*
> *There I cowch when Owles doe crie,*
> *On the Batts backe I doe flie*
> > *after Sommer merrily.*
> *Merrily, merrily, shall I liue now,*
> *Vnder the blossom that hangs on the Bow.*

Pro. Why that's my dainty *Ariell*: I shall misse
Thee, but yet thou shalt haue freedome: so, so, so.
To the Kings ship, inuisible as thou art,
There shalt thou finde the Marriners asleepe
Vnder the Hatches: the Master and the Boat-swaine
Being awake, enforce them to this place;
And presently, I pre'thee.

Ar. I drinke the aire before me, and returne
Or ere your pulse twice beate.   *Exit.*

Gon. All torment, trouble, wonder, and amazement
Inhabits heere: some heauenly power guide vs
Out of this fearefull Country.

Pro. Behold Sir King
The wronged Duke of *Millaine*, *Prospero*:
For more assurance that a liuing Prince
Do's now speake to thee, I embrace thy body,
And to thee, and thy Company, I bid

A hearty welcome.

Alo. Where thou bee'st he or no,
Or some inchanted trifle to abuse me,
(As late I haue beene) I not know: thy Pulse
Beats as of flesh, and blood: and since I saw thee,
Th'affliction of my minde amends, with which
I feare a madnesse held me: this must craue
(And if this be at all) a most strange story.
Thy Dukedome I resigne, and doe entreat
Thou pardon me my wrongs: But how shold *Prospero*
Be liuing, and be heere?

Pro. First, noble Frend,
Let me embrace thine age, whose honor cannot
Be measur'd, or confin'd.

Gonz. Whether this be,
Or be not, I'le not sweare.

Pro. You doe yet taste
Some subtleties o'th'Isle, that will nor let you
Beleeue things certaine: Wellcome, my friends all,
But you, my brace of Lords, were I so minded
I heere could plucke his Highnesse frowne vpon you
And iustifie you Traitors: at this time
I will tell no tales.

Seb. The Diuell speakes in him:

Pro. No:
For you (most wicked Sir) whom to call brother
Would euen infect my mouth, I do forgiue
Thy rankest fault; all of them: and require
My Dukedome of thee, which, perforce I know
Thou must restore.

Alo. If thou beest *Prospero*
Giue vs particulars of thy preseruation,

How thou hast met vs heere, whom three howres since
Were wrackt vpon this shore? where I haue lost
(How sharp the point of this remembrance is)
My deere sonne *Ferdinand*.

  Pro. I am woe for't, Sir.

  Alo. Irreparable is the losse, and patience
Saies, it is past her cure.

  Pro. I rather thinke
You haue not sought her helpe, of whose soft grace
For the like losse, I haue her soueraigne aid,
And rest my selfe content.

  Alo. You the like losse?

  Pro. As great to me, as late, and supportable
To make the deere losse, haue I meanes much weaker
Then you may call to comfort you; for I
Haue lost my daughter.

  Alo. A daughter?
Oh heauens, that they were liuing both in *Nalpes*
The King and Queene there, that they were, I wish
My selfe were mudded in that oo-zie bed
Where my sonne lies: when did you lose your daughter?

  Pro. In this last Tempest. I perceiue these Lords
At this encounter doe so much admire,
That they deuoure their reason, and scarce thinke
Their eies doe offices of Truth: Their words
Are naturall breath: but howsoeu'r you haue
Beene iustled from your sences, know for certain
That I am *Prospero*, and that very Duke
Which was thrust forth of *Millaine*, who most strangely
Vpon this shore (where you were wrackt) was landed
To be the Lord on't: No more yet of this,
For 'tis a Chronicle of day by day,

Not a relation for a break-fast, nor
Befitting this first meeting: Welcome, Sir;
This Cell's my Court: heere haue I few attendants,
And Subiects none abroad: pray you looke in:
My Dukedome since you haue giuen me againe,
I will requite you with as good a thing,
At least bring forth a wonder, to content ye
As much, as me my Dukedome.

Here Prospero discouers Ferdinand and Miranda,
playing at Chesse.

Mir. Sweet Lord, you play me false.

Fer. No my dearest loue,
I would not for the world.

Mir. Yes, for a score of Kingdomes, you should wrangle,
And I would call it faire play.

Alo. If this proue
A vision of the Island, one deere Sonne
Shall I twice loose.

Seb. A most high miracle.

Fer. Though the Seas threaten they are mercifull,
I haue curs'd them without cause.

Alo. Now all the blessings
Of a glad father, compasse thee about:
Arise, and say how thou cam'st heere.

Mir. O wonder!
How many goodly creatures are there heere?
How beauteous mankinde is? O braue new world
That has such people in't.

Pro. 'Tis new to thee.

Alo. What is this Maid, with whom thou was't at play?
Your eld'st acquaintance cannot be three houres:
Is she the goddesse that hath seuer'd vs,

And brought vs thus together?

Fer. Sir, she is mortall;
But by immortall prouidence, she's mine;
I chose her when I could not aske my Father
For his aduise: nor thought I had one: She
Is daughter to this famous Duke of *Millaine*,
Of whom, so often I haue heard renowne,
But neuer saw before: of whom I haue
Receiu'd a second life; and second Father
This Lady makes him to me.

Alo. I am hers.
But O, how odly will it sound, that I
Must aske my childe forgiuenesse?

Pro. There Sir stop,
Let vs not burthen our remembrances, with
A heauinesse that's gon.

Gon. I haue inly wept,
Or should haue spoke ere this: looke downe you gods
And on this couple drop a blessed crowne;
For it is you, that haue chalk'd forth the way
Which brought vs hither.

Alo. I say Amen, *Gonzallo*.

Gon. Was *Millaine* thrust from *Millaine*, that his Issue
Should become Kings of *Naples*? O reioyce
Beyond a common ioy, and set it downe
With gold on lasting Pillers: In one voyage
Did *Claribell* her husband finde at *Tunis*,
And *Ferdinand* her brother, found a wife,
Where he himselfe was lost: *Prospero*, his Dukedome
In a poore Isle: and all of vs, our selues,
When no man was his owne.

Alo. Giue me your hands:

Let griefe and sorrow still embrace his heart,
That doth not wish you ioy.

    Gon. Be it so, Amen.

               Enter Ariell, with the Master and Boatswaine
                    amazedly following.

O looke Sir, looke Sir, here is more of vs:
I prophesi'd, if a Gallowes were on Land
This fellow could not drowne: Now blasphemy,
That swear'st Grace ore-boord, not an oath on shore,
Hast thou no mouth by land?
What is the newes?

    Bot. The best newes is, that we haue safely found
Our King, and company: The next: our Ship,
Which but three glasses since, we gaue out split,
Is tyte, and yare, and brauely rig'd, as when
We first put out to Sea.

    Ar. Sir, all this seruice
Haue I done since I went.

    Pro. My tricksey Spirit.

    Alo. These are not naturall euents, they strengthen
From strange, to stranger: say, how came you hither?

    Bot. If I did thinke, Sir, I were well awake,
I'ld striue to tell you: we were dead of sleepe,
And (how we know not) all clapt vnder hatches,
Where, but euen now, with strange, and seuerall noyses
Of roring, shreeking, howling, gingling chaines,
And mo diuersitie of sounds, all horrible.
We were awak'd: straight way, at liberty;
Where we, in all our trim, freshly beheld
Our royall, good, and gallant Ship: our Master
Capring to eye her: on a trice, so please you,
Euen in a dreame, were we diuided from them,

And were brought moaping hither.

Ar. Was't well done?

Pro. Brauely (my diligence) thou shalt be free.

Alo. This is as strange a Maze, as ere men trod,
And there is in this businesse, more then nature
Was euer conduct of: some Oracle
Must rectifie our knowledge.

Pro. Sir, my Leige,
Doe not infest your minde, with beating on
The strangenesse of this businesse, at pickt leisure
(Which shall be shortly single) I'le resolue you,
(Which to you shall seeme probable) of euery
These happend accidents: till when, be cheerefull
And thinke of each thing well: Come hither Spirit,
Set *Caliban*, and his companions free:
Vntye the Spell: How fares my gracious Sir?
There are yet missing of your Companie
Some few odde Lads, that you remember not.

> *Enter Ariell, driuing in Caliban, Stephano,*
> *and Trinculo in their stolne Apparell.*

Ste. Euery man shift for all the rest, and let
No man take care for himselfe; for all is
But fortune: *Coragio* Bully-Monster *Corasio*.

Tri. If these be true spies which I weare in my head, here's
a goodly sight.

Cal. O *Setebos*, these be braue Spirits indeede:
How fine my Master is? I am afraid
He will chastise me.

Seb. Ha, ha:
What things are these, my Lord *Anthonio*?
Will money buy em?

Ant. Very like: one of them

Is a plaine Fish, and no doubt marketable.

Pro. Marke but the badges of these men, my Lords,
Then say if they be true: This mishapen knaue;
His Mother was a Witch, and one so strong
That could controle the Moone; make flowes, and ebs,
And deale in her command, without her power:
These three haue robd me, and this demy-diuell;
(For he's a bastard one) had plotted with them
To take my life: two of these Fellowes, you
Must know, and owne, this Thing of darkenesse, I
Acknowledge mine.

Cal. I shall be pincht to death.

Alo. Is not this *Stephano*, my drunken Butler?

Seb. He is drunke now;
Where had he wine?

Alo. And *Trinculo* is reeling ripe: where should they
Finde this grand Liquor that hath gilded 'em?
How cam'st thou in this pickle?

Tri. I haue bin in such a pickle since I saw you last,
That I feare me will neuer out of my bones:
I shall not feare fly-blowing.

Seb. Why how now *Stephano?*

Ste. O touch me not, I am not *Stephano*, but a Cramp.

Pro. You'ld be King o'the Isle, Sirha?

Ste. I should haue bin a sore one then.

Alo. This is a strange thing as ere I look'd on.

Pro. He is as disproportion'd in his Manners
As in his shape: Goe Sirha, to my Cell,
Take with you your Companions: as you looke
To haue my pardon, trim it handsomely.

Cal. I that I will: and Ile be wise hereafter,
And seeke for grace: what a thrice double Asse

Was I to take this drunkard for a god?
And worship this dull foole?

   Pro. Goe to, away.

   Alo. Hence, and bestow your luggage where you found it.

   Seb. Or stole it rather.

   Pro. Sir, I inuite your Highnesse, and your traine
To my poore Cell: where you shall take your rest
For this one night, which part of it, Ile waste
With such discourse, as I not doubt, shall make it
Goe quicke away: The story of my life,
And the particular accidents, gon by
Since I came to this Isle: And in the morne
I'le bring you to your ship, and so to *Naples*,
Where I haue hope to see the nuptiall
Of these our deere-belou'd, solemnized,
And thence retire me to my *Millaine*, where
Euery third thought shall be my graue.

   Alo. I long
To heare the story of your life; which must
Take the eare starngely.

   Pro. I'le deliuer all,
And promise you calme Seas, auspicious gales,
And saile, so expeditious, that shall catch
Your Royall fleete farre off: My *Ariel*; chicke
That is thy charge: Then to the Elements
Be free, and fare thou well: please you draw neere.

                             Exeunt omnes.

EPILOGVE,
spoken by *Prospero*.

Now my Charmes are all ore-throwne,
And what strength I haue's mine owne.
Which is most faint: now 'tis true
I must be heere confinde by you,
Or sent to Naples, *Let me not*
Since I haue my Dukedome got,
And pardon'd the deceiuer, dwell
In this bare Island, by your Spell,
But release me from my bands
With the helpe of your good hands:
Gentle breath of yours, my Sailes
Must fill, or else my proiect failes,
Which was to please: Now I want
Spirits to enforce: Art to inchant,
And my ending is despaire,
Vnlesse I be relieu'd by praier
Which pierces so, that it assaults
Mercy it selfe, and frees all faults.
  As you from crimes would pardon'd be,
  Let your Indulgence set me free.   Exit.

The Scene, an vn-inhabited Island
Names of the Actors.

Alonso, K. of Naples:
Sebastian his Brother.
Prospero, the right Duke of Millaine.
Anthonio his brother, the vsurping Duke of Millaine.
Ferdinand, Son to the King of Naples.
Gonzalo, an honest old Councellor.
Adrian, & Francisco, Lords.
Caliban, a saluage and deformed slaue.
Trinculo, a Iester.
Stephano, a drunken Butler.
Master of a Ship.
Boate-Swaine.
Marriners.
Miranda, daughter to Prospero.
Ariell, an ayrie spirit.
Iris
Ceres
Iuno   } *Spirits.*
Nymphes
Reapers

FINIS.